# THE
# AMISH

**STAR QUILT**
c. 1848–50
*Holmes County, Ohio*

**LIZZIE'S FRIENDSHIP QUILT**
c. 1899
*Topeka, Indiana*

**DIAMOND QUILT**
c. 1895
*Lancaster County, Pennsylvania*

**OCEAN WAVES QUILT**
c. 1901
*Ligonier, Indiana*

**DOUBLE CHAIN QUILT**
c. 1910
*Pennsylvania*

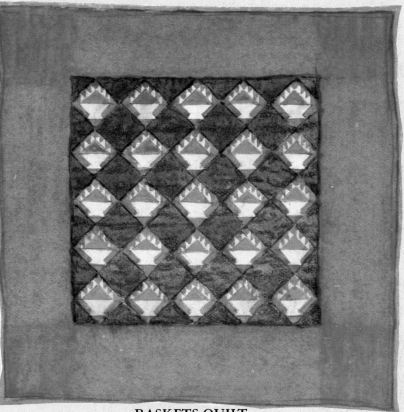

**BASKETS QUILT**
c. 1910
*Pennsylvania*

**DIAMOND QUILT**
c. 1900
*Lancaster County, Pennsylvania*

**SUNSHINE AND SHADOW QUILT**
c. 1870
*Lancaster County, Pennsylvania*

# THE
# AMISH

## Doris Faber
### Illustrated by
## Michael E. Erkel

Doubleday
New York London Toronto Sydney Auckland

Special thanks to Stephen Scott of
"The People's Place," an
educational center for the Amish
and Mennonite community in
Lancaster, Pennsylvania, for his
careful review of the manuscript
and illustrations.

Published by Doubleday,
a division of Bantam Doubleday Dell
Publishing Group, Inc.,
666 Fifth Avenue, New York,
New York 10103
Doubleday
and the portrayal of an anchor with a
dolphin are trademarks of Doubleday, a
division of Bantam Doubleday Dell
Publishing Group, Inc.

Library of Congress Cataloging-in-
Publication Data
Faber, Doris, 1924–
    The Amish / Doris Faber ;
illustrated by Michael E. Erkel. — 1st
ed.      p.   cm.
    Summary: Discusses the history,
culture, daily lifestyle, and future of the
Amish people.
    Includes index.
    1. Amish—United States—Juvenile
literature. [1. Amish.]
I. Erkel, Michael E., ill.  II. Title.
E184.M45F37   1991
973'.08287—dc20   89-7829   CIP   AC
ISBN 0-385-26130-6
ISBN 0-385-26131-4 (lib. bdg.)
RL: 3.6
Copyright © 1991 by Doris Faber
Illustrations copyright © 1991 by
Michael E. Erkel
All Rights Reserved '
Printed in Italy
February 1991
First Edition

# Who Are They?

A bus filled with tourists has just turned off the main highway onto this narrow country road. As it rolls past peaceful farms, the people on it stare out of their windows—at tidy squares of green, and a few clusters of trim white buildings. Then something on the road ahead makes the driver of the big bus slow down suddenly.

It's a little black buggy, swaying behind a clip-clopping horse. The man holding the reins and the boy beside him both are wearing old-fashioned straw hats with a band of black ribbon right above the wide brim.

So they must be Amish!

A buzz of eager interest stirs among the tourists. But some of them feel uneasy, too, as a new thought strikes them. What must it be like to have busloads of strangers always peering at you?

A college research team that was allowed to make a study of Amish (AH-mish) life received this answer from one man: "I just don't enjoy living in a museum or a zoo, whatever you would call it."

That's why many of the Amish who live in areas that attract a lot of tourists try not to go into town during the summer or on weekends. Yet even if they shy away from prying eyes, they are not unfriendly. They make very good neighbors, according to other residents of the rural parts of Pennsylvania, Ohio and Indiana where the largest Amish communities are located.

All over the country, though, people have been feeling more sympathy with the Amish. Until recent years, most Americans knew very little about them —except that their strict religion kept them from using any modern conveniences, such as cars or electric lights. So they were often pitied or made fun of. Also, because their religion made them refuse to obey some laws, they were sometimes treated as criminals.

But opinions about the Amish have been changing for several reasons. As the result of efforts by other minorities to win fair treatment, the average person is less likely to look down on those who follow their own rules. What's more, many Americans feel that modern ways may be harming our environment. In the words of a young Pennsylvania neighbor of the Amish: "It's not so weird to live a simple life now."

This new outlook has led television and movies to further spread a favorable image of the Amish. So some Amish people have noticed that nowadays tourists often seem too admiring.

"They think we are angels or better than other people," an Amish minister told one writer, "and they expect to find us floating several feet above the ground."

Instead, today's Amish are really quite a bit like the rest of us—even though they uphold a religion that deeply influences their daily lives. Because they believe that people benefit more from hard work than amusement, they never watch television. Because they disapprove of giving special attention to any individual, they don't even want other people to take pictures of them. Despite computers and space capsules, they keep clip-clopping along in their horse-drawn buggies.

But what makes them continue to follow all of these rules that set them apart so much?

# Back in Europe

A long time ago, during the 1500s, Europe was torn by wars about religion. Those were the years when most of today's Protestant groups were formed. For instance, a strong-minded leader named Martin Luther started a new church—and his followers became known as Lutherans.

Another group was led by a Dutch preacher whose ideas aroused strong opposition in many countries. His name was Menno Simons. So his followers were called *Mennonites.*

The Mennonites wanted to make religion simpler. They felt that too many changes had been made since the days of the earliest Christians, and they aimed to give up everything that had been added. But one of their beliefs struck other people as very dangerous.

The Mennonites believed that it was wrong to baptize infants. Instead, they held that baptism should be saved for individuals old enough to understand its meaning—for young men and women around the age of eighteen. Surprising as it may seem today, Mennonites who refused to let their babies be baptized were often arrested, tortured or even killed.

This harsh treatment made Mennonites flee to several other countries of Europe. Everywhere, they tried to avoid trouble by holding their prayer meetings secretly—in people's homes, rather than a church. But violence against them still broke out repeatedly.

Faced by so many enemies, some Mennonites found comfort when a new

leader began preaching a stern message. He urged an even stricter obedience to the teachings of Jesus, not merely on religious matters. He also said that only very plain clothing should be worn, and that men should never trim their beards.

His name was Jacob Amman. Those who heeded his words at first were called Amish Mennonites, then over the years this was shortened to just the Amish.

Hardly anything is known about Jacob Amman himself, apart from the fact that he had been born in Switzerland. Late in the 1600s, he did most of his preaching in the Alsace region of present-day France, an area then under German rule. So most of the original Amish spoke German as their native language.

They were mainly rural folk. Hardworking farmers, they would have contentedly tilled the soil and worshiped according to their own beliefs—if they had not faced increasing danger from their neighbors.

As waves of arrest came more and more often, terrible stories about Amish who had been tortured made some members of the group drop out. But the most convinced believers could not give up their religion. Nor could they fight against their enemies, because one of their basic beliefs forbade them to take part in any sort of violence.

The most devoted of the Amish chose instead to flee again—hoping to find religious freedom, at last, in the New World.

# To America

**I**t was 1737. In the Dutch seaport of Rotterdam, a ship going to America waited for fair weather. On this ship—named *Charming Nancy*—were the first Amish families known to have left Europe.

Perhaps a few other families might have come a little earlier, but there are no records of their trip. On the *Charming Nancy,* though, an Amish man kept a diary. Because parts of his diary have been saved, we can be sure that sailing on this ship with such a cheerful name was really a horrible experience.

The Amish were packed "as closely as herring." Also, bad food and water caused much sickness, especially among the children. More than a dozen children and several adults died during the voyage.

The diary does not say anything about the feelings of its writer. But we can guess what he must have felt when he wrote:

Landed in Philadelphia on the 18th of September and my wife and I left the ship on the 19th. A child was born to us on the 20th—died—wife recovered. A voyage of 83 days.

Still, the Amish who did reach Philadelphia found much to be thankful for. So other believers soon came to join them. About five hundred Amish men, women and children left Europe during the 1700s, and about three thousand more during the 1800s.

Since the European Amish had no churches where records might have been saved, nobody can say how many people had belonged to the different branches of the religion there. Yet the number cannot have been very large. By the time Amish families stopped coming to America—around 1860— only a few believers remained on the other side of the ocean. Today, no Amish at all live in the lands where the group started.

There were several reasons for this complete disappearance. Even though the Old World Amish were sometimes allowed to live in peace, they could not live the way they wished. Because a large part of Europe's land belonged to the owners of enormous estates, it was almost impossible for poor farm workers ever to buy their own farms. So most of the Amish only rented land. And they had to obey all sorts of hateful rules set by their landlords.

But, in the New World, things were very different. Religious liberty was the policy of some of the English colonies, even before the American Revolution brought the founding of the United States. What's more, plenty of land was available. So conditions were ideal for a group like the Amish.

The first Amish to arrive in America settled not far from Philadelphia, where other German-speaking followers of less strict religions already lived.

Since the German word for the language they spoke was *Deutsch*—which sounded like "Dutch" to the English—this area soon became known as the Pennsylvania Dutch country.

Later waves of Amish usually landed in New Orleans, and from there it was easy to sail up the Mississippi River to midwestern farming districts. That was why most of the Amish who crossed the ocean during the 1800s settled in Ohio or Indiana.

Most of today's Amish still live in the same three states. But there are also Amish communities in seventeen other states as well as the Canadian province of Ontario. Over the years, the population of all these settlements has kept on growing—reaching, by the late 1980s, a total of about 100,000.

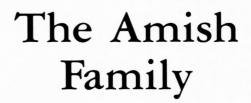

# The Amish Family

Everything the Amish do is centered around their homes. Their work and their worship, their weddings and their funerals, all take place right where they live. So the family is their basic unit.

The most important fact about the Amish family—which largely explains why the group's population has kept increasing—is that its members look on children as a great blessing, and they have a lot of them. Among the Amish, the average home has seven children, with ten or even fifteen not uncommon.

As a result, Amish boys and girls grow up surrounded by relatives. Besides their own brothers and sisters, many cousins usually live nearby. Often their grandparents do, too, perhaps in a separate wing of the same house.

Until Amish babies are about two years old, they are treated very tenderly. Loved as gifts from God, they receive much care and almost never are alone. Even when they fret, only mild discipline is considered necessary.

But once Amish children can walk and talk, they are expected to obey their parents without question. Any refusal to do as they are told is likely to be punished by a spanking. But really harsh treatment is not allowed by the Amish religion.

Little children in Amish families also are expected to do simple chores around the farm or in the kitchen. From their earliest years, boys are taught to help their fathers and girls their mothers. For the Amish hold that the proper role of women is to take care of their homes and children, while men support their families. So the training of Amish youngsters prepares them to follow this traditional division of labor.

Beyond sitting still at lengthy Sunday prayer meetings, though, neither boys nor girls have any religious duties during their childhood. At the

one-room Amish schools where they learn reading, writing and arithmetic, they also learn the teachings of the Amish religion—they sing Amish hymns and recite Amish prayers. Yet they are not really members of the church until they are baptized, usually soon after they turn eighteen.

But don't they ever just have fun?

Ride past an Amish school during the noon recess, and you will see a yard filled with boys and girls. They seem not very different from any other youngsters—even though they look as if they might be out of an old-time movie. All the girls have their hair pinned into granny-type buns at the back of their neck, and they are wearing plain dark dresses. The boys have on rather wide black pants held up by black suspenders. Still, many of the children are playing a game of hide-and-seek. Under a tree, there are swings for others to enjoy.

Also, when Amish youth reach their mid-teens, they have a special dating time. It's called "rumspringa," or running around. Then they are encouraged to gather Sunday evenings to sing lively songs. The singing leads to pairing-off for buggy rides and other outings, even to parties not much different from teenage parties outside the Amish community.

For many Amish parents believe in giving their young people a taste of freedom before they settle down to raise families of their own. Strict as some of their rules are, they let their children decide by themselves whom they want to marry. Nobody else is even supposed to suspect that a wedding is planned until it's announced at a religious service just a few weeks in advance.

Yet the Amish like to gossip as much as other people do. If a family plants extra rows of celery in its garden, tongues begin to wag. Because a lot of celery is needed when the stuffing is prepared for the many chickens and ducks served at a wedding feast, neighbors guess immediately that a daughter of this family will soon wed.

# Model Farmers

**R**ight from their earliest days in Europe, the Amish were very good farmers. Their fields always looked well tended, and their harvests often were bigger than those of their non-Amish neighbors.

For one of the basic Amish aims is to live in harmony with nature. They believe that cultivating the soil has a deep religious meaning. As a result, work that others might consider drudgery gives them a great sense of inner peace.

But back when everybody drove around in horse-drawn buggies, the Amish way of running their farms did not really differ much from the practices of other good farmers. Beyond growing food to feed their own families, they all thought that taking care of their land was more important than anything else. So they used animal manure as fertilizer, and they planted varied crops to keep their fields from wearing out.

Then tractors and other machines brought big changes. Most farmers began using machines to grow much more food with much less work. The Amish, though, still kept using teams of horses instead of tractors. Soon their farms came to seem just like pretty pictures from the distant past.

However, in recent years the "modernizing" of farm areas has

speeded up. All over the country, thousands of small farms have disappeared—replaced by fewer, larger farms, along with a lot of new houses or shopping malls. For several reasons, this worries some people.

Does it make sense, in the long run, to use so much oil to run farm machines? How much harm to the environment has been caused by modern farming practices? Will future generations suffer because so much good farmland is being paved over with highways? Questions like these have lately stirred up a new interest in old-fashioned Amish farms.

Yet at the same time that the Amish are gaining more respect as model farmers, they themselves face increasing problems. Because they can't possibly produce everything they need with their own hands, they must earn enough money to buy shoes and other items for their large families. Most important of all, their religion holds that it's their duty to help their grown children buy land on which to begin farming independently.

But the price of land has kept going up higher and higher. So the Amish

have been forced to consider new ways for increasing their income. Even if the use of machinery is still frowned on by the strictest branches of the group, most others have found it possible to make some compromises.

For instance, they use gasoline or diesel engines to provide power in their barns for milking machines. In some Amish communities, even tractors are permitted for fieldwork. By and large, only electricity carried to homes by overhead wires remains totally unacceptable.

The biggest change, though, is that a growing number of Amish are no longer farmers. Because of the high price of land almost half the young men in some Amish communities now work at other trades, such as carpentry or blacksmithing. They aim to set up their own shops on their own property. But more and more of them are finding it necessary to seek jobs in small factories near their settlements.

Some Amish women, too, work for "the English." (Because members of the group still speak German among themselves, that's the way they refer to all outsiders.)

# "Judge not . . ."

It wasn't uncommon, even in the old days, for Amish girls to work a few years as mother's helpers. When they were around sixteen, they took jobs in the homes of "the English" and saved their pay, to use it when they set up homes of their own. Today, some Amish women earn money by sewing handmade quilts, selling plants at garden shops or cooking in restaurant kitchens.

So every Amish family is likely to have many contacts with outsiders. Even though the rules of their religion affect the way they themselves live, they have never been required to separate themselves entirely from other people. Since they are known as hard workers who can be relied on, employers like to hire them—especially because they never try to convince anybody else that the Amish way is superior.

Down through history, many religious groups have felt so sure about their own beliefs that they considered it their duty to convert non-believers. But the Amish believe that no individual should ever take on the right to decide the proper course for another person.

This belief is based on some words from the Bible that the Amish value highly. The words, which help to explain their whole outlook, are: "Judge not, that ye be not judged."

# Buttons and Brims

To the eyes of outsiders, Amish buggies probably all look alike. It seems that every member of the group wears the same kind of clothing and follows the same rules. Among the Amish themselves, though, many differences are clear—and fine points, such as the exact width of a hat brim, have a special meaning to them.

Amish clothing for both men and women is very much like what most people wore hundreds of years ago in the parts of Europe where the group started. Those who adopted the Amish religion gave up all sorts of bright trimmings, but otherwise they dressed the way their non-Amish neighbors did.

Of course, the Amish decision to forbid ribbons and bows was a sign that their religion opposed human vanity. Their preachers held that simple clothing showed the humble spirit they should be cultivating. But as time went on, other people's newer styles of dressing reflected the changing world around them. Then the fact that the Amish kept to their old style gained new importance.

The Amish considered the new fashions taken up by outsiders as *symbols* of worldly civilization that must be avoided. So they put increasing value on their own symbols, from buttons to buggies. Small details—for instance, the exact shape of a woman's cape or the number of pleats on a young girl's cap—came to have a particular significance to them.

Even so, most of these symbols have

Work Clothing

Church Clothing

been changed at least slightly over the years. Although outsiders may think that the Amish oppose every type of change, in fact the truth is more complicated. There are really two kinds of rules governing the religion's believers.

Basic religious ideas dating back several hundred years remain the same for the Amish, generation after generation. But rules regarding daily life are set by each Amish district, containing twenty to forty families. Rules of this type do change, if only slowly.

Still, a lot of differences have developed during recent years. As might be expected, the strictest believers have changed the least. And the Amish can tell which branch of the religion a man belongs to just by glancing at his hat—the wider the brim, the stricter his opinions are sure to be.

Sometimes there are far more noticeable changes. For instance, several Amish communities in Pennsylvania had problems about the shoes their children were required to wear. Perhaps the traditional high black shoes became too expensive. Or maybe even Amish children rebelled against wearing these shoes.

At any rate, if you look carefully to see what Amish girls and boys in their school yard are wearing on their feet, you may be surprised. Many of them— and nowadays, even many of their mothers—have on ordinary gray or even purple-striped running sneakers!

# A Great Controversy

Suppose your family belonged to an Amish community that agreed to allow the wearing of sneakers—but your father deeply disapproved of this decision. In his mind, old-style black shoes remained an important symbol of religious faith.

This sort of disagreement, about shoes or tractors, has come up more often than outsiders might suspect. Because the Amish religion does not permit open dispute over any question, nobody else knows when there has been a difference of opinion. Those who object to a change approved by most of their neighbors must either accept the change or join another community with views like their own.

Following this policy of moving, rather than fighting, like-minded Amish sometimes set up new communities in areas far away from existing settlements. Although the shortage of land for young families is usually given as the reason for starting new colonies, differences in outlook probably spur even more movement.

Still, the main issue affecting the Amish during the recent past put the whole group on the same side. *Could any state force Amish parents to send their boys and girls to public schools?* It took the United States Supreme Court to settle the great controversy this question raised.

Until the 1950s, most Amish children did attend the same schools as their non-Amish neighbors—usually, one-room schools just a short walk from their homes. The simple lessons in these schools fit in with the Amish belief that their children should be taught only the basic subjects of reading, writing and arithmetic. Also, the Amish felt comforted by the fact that their older children were learning right in the same room as their younger children, and could always watch over them.

But the new trend toward combining rural school districts, then building large central schools, struck the Amish as a dangerous threat. They strongly opposed having their children ride many miles by bus to a big school where they would have to study subjects with no bearing on their future lives. Amish parents feared that the new system would tear their children away from their religion.

So Amish communities began starting small schools of their own. Often, these were in the very buildings that used to be local public schools.

Yet these Amish schools could not satisfy some of the requirements set by state departments of education. For instance, Amish teachers lacked the advanced training needed to earn a teaching certificate. What's more, no teacher acceptable to the Amish could earn such a certificate—because the religion firmly forbids all higher education.

The result was a series of very emotional scenes. In some states, police went so far as to force Amish children onto school buses while their parents stood by weeping and praying. Because of the Amish rule against any type of protest—even the filing of a lawsuit—members of the group had only one step they could take.

Many Amish families in the areas where the trouble broke out just packed up and moved away. They went to other states where they hoped they would be let alone. But in some places, Amish fathers were sent to prison because of their refusal to send their children to public schools.

Meanwhile, though, concerned citizens with no Amish ties began holding meetings. They formed the National Committee for Amish Religious Freedom. It was this group that started a test case about the policy of forcing Amish children to attend public schools.

Finally, on May 15, 1972, the Supreme Court decided, by a vote of 7–0, in favor of the Amish. The verdict was based on the First Amendment to the Constitution, protecting all Americans against interference with their religious liberty.

Announcing the Court's decision, Chief Justice Warren Burger made two points. He said that states surely had the right to see that their children got a good education. But, he added, this "must be measured against" the right of all Americans to enjoy religious freedom.

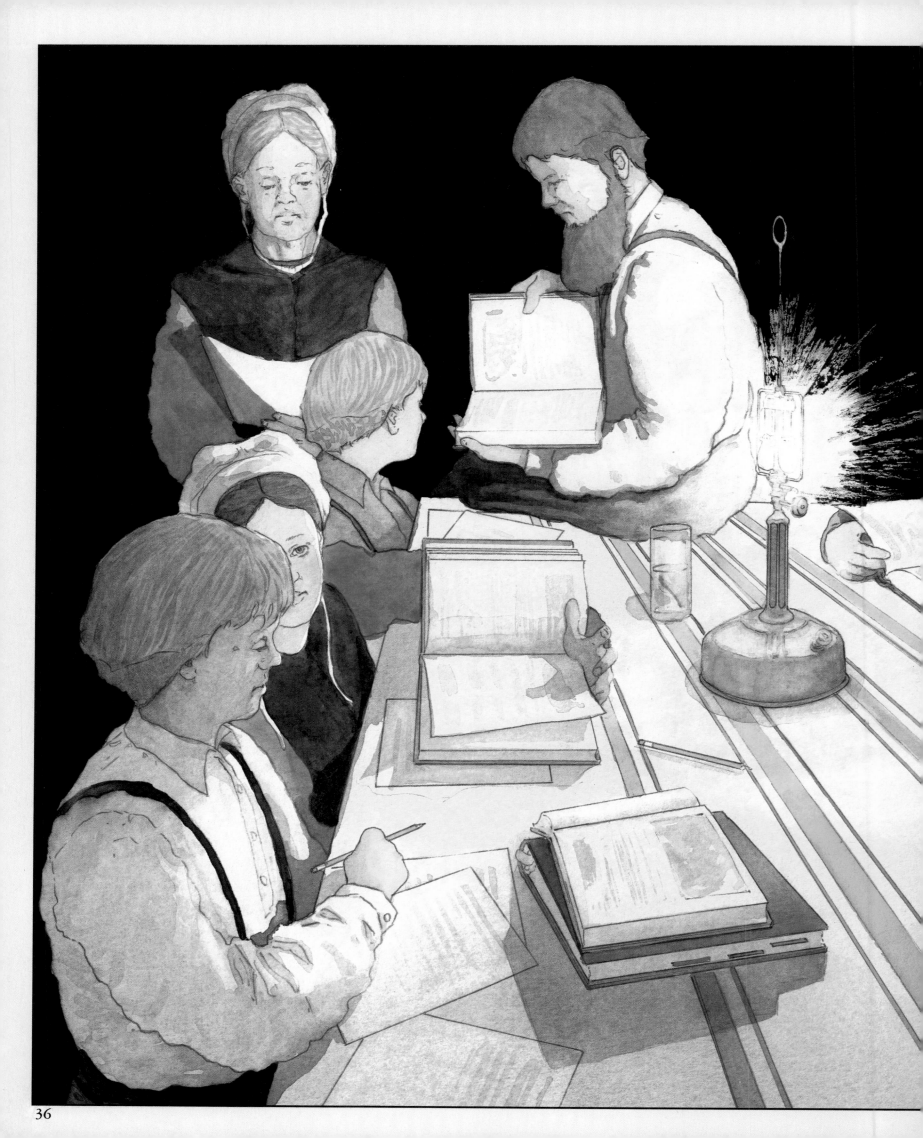

# New Pressures

The Supreme Court victory of the Amish was very important. After it, no law that said all children must attend public schools could be enforced —if it interfered with the religious beliefs of any group.

As far as the Amish themselves were concerned, the verdict happily ended a long period of stress. Still, many Amish leaders and state educational officials had to arrive at compromises on several specific points. For instance, the Amish agreed that teachers in their own schools would attend meetings to become familiar with state-approved teaching practices. And the officials gave up insisting that Amish young people must have high school training until the age of sixteen.

Instead, older children could take a sort of vocational course—with only an hour or so a week of actual school attendance required. The students could spend the rest of the time helping out at home and then writing reports on their activities.

So the greatest controversy ever to involve the Amish was settled.

However, other complications of modern life keep causing new tensions between the Amish and the different levels of American government.

Always, the Amish have tried to obey local and national laws. Even though they will neither vote nor hold any office themselves, they accept the fact that governments are necessary. They pay taxes and willingly help to support volunteer fire companies or disaster relief efforts. Despite their hatred for war, Amish men have signed up when military drafts were in effect. Claiming the status of conscientious objectors, they worked in hospitals or at other non-combat duty.

Still, Amish buggies are bound to cause traffic tie-ups, as even country roads get crowded. And any change affecting one of the group's main symbols is resisted by strict believers. So new laws that require buggies to have bright orange markers—making it easier for motorists to see them—are accepted only slowly.

Also, when Pennsylvania wanted to build a new highway cutting off many Amish farms from their neighbors, dozens of buggies parked in silent protest outside the building where a hearing on the plan was being held. For the Amish consider it part of their religious duty to live close to each other, so that each member of a community can easily help any other.

This Amish insistence on taking care of their own in their own way causes much of the friction that develops from time to time between the Amish and "the English."

However, there are no Amish doctors —because of the religion's ban on higher education. When Amish people get sick, they go to "English" doctors in their area who understand the group's rules. Also, most Amish babies are born in hospitals. But if medical service for home births is available, the Amish would much rather use it.

Otherwise, the Amish try to deal with life's ups and downs on their own as much as possible. They don't believe in accepting any sort of payments from the government, even Social Security benefits when they get old.

Back in the 1960s, several Amish men took the unusual step of going to Washington. There, they spoke up at a hearing and explained that they considered it a religious duty to take care of their old relatives without any outside help. Then Congress passed a new law, allowing self-employed Amish not to pay any Social Security tax.

# Survival?

On a sunny September morning, about one hundred and fifty Amish men are taking part in a time-honored tradition.

It's a barn raising. Some weeks earlier, a fire caused by lightning had destroyed an Amish barn along with all the hay that it contained. Now the charred remains have been cleared away, and volunteers using only basic tools such as handsaws and hammers will put up a fine new barn before this day is over. Then they will fill it with hay donated by neighbors.

While the men are putting together the frame for the new building, Amish women prepare the lunch and supper that will be served at long tables right in the yard. Children flit everywhere, doing errands for their elders or playing simple games. The entire picture has the appealing charm of a simpler era.

But how much longer can the simplicity of Amish life survive in today's complex world?

Back around 1950, many people thought that all the benefits of modern civilization were bound to lure increasing numbers of Amish away

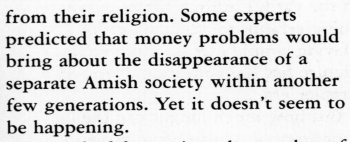

from their religion. Some experts predicted that money problems would bring about the disappearance of a separate Amish society within another few generations. Yet it doesn't seem to be happening.

Instead of decreasing, the number of Amish communities appears to be growing. According to the best available figures, down through the years about 20 percent of the children born to Amish families dropped out of the group around the time they were eligible to be baptized or soon afterward. Nowadays, the percentage of dropouts continues to be almost the same. But because the Amish have such large families, their total population actually has been increasing at a faster rate than almost any other category of Americans.

Despite these figures, some admirers of the Amish way of life still worry that the group won't be able to keep on thriving much longer. They point to newspaper stories about rowdy parties held by Amish teenagers, or about Amish young people who wreck cars that their parents didn't even know they owned.

Even so, most Amish young people do accept the strict discipline of their religion when they must choose whether or not to be baptized. They make this choice mainly because the deep sense of belonging that Amish life provides is more important to them than whatever pleasures they must give up to remain members.

As one professor put it:

"Amish society will survive—if it keeps giving the children raised in Amish homes the feeling that their way of life will give them more inner contentment than any other way can offer."

# Index

## About the Author

Doris Faber is an established author of nonfiction for children with more than forty titles to her credit. She graduated from New York University and later became a reporter for *The New York Times* where she met and married a fellow reporter. The couple eventually left the *Times* to raise a family and write books.

The author now lives on a farm in upstate New York, with her husband and frequent co-author, Harold.

## About the Artist

Michael E. Erkel is a talented young artist who lives with his wife and four children in the Blue Ridge Mountains of Virginia. The Erkel family not only share in the responsibilities of a small farm but also contribute to the interesting projects Mr. Erkel undertakes. Be it painting murals or designing children's furniture, everyone's ideas and participation are welcome. Because of the artist's own rural setting and sense of family life, this book was a particular pleasure for him to illustrate and one in which he could portray the Amish in a realistic light.

**STAR QUILT**
c. 1848–50
*Holmes County, Ohio*

**LIZZIE'S FRIENDSHIP QUILT**
c. 1899
*Topeka, Indiana*

**DIAMOND QUILT**
c. 1895
*Lancaster County, Pennsylvania*

**OCEAN WAVES QUILT**
c. 1901
*Ligonier, Indiana*

**DOUBLE CHAIN QUILT**
c. 1910
*Pennsylvania*

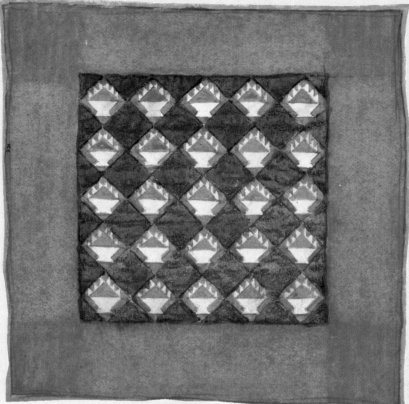

**BASKETS QUILT**
c. 1910
*Pennsylvania*

**DIAMOND QUILT**
c. 1900
*Lancaster County, Pennsylvania*

**SUNSHINE AND SHADOW QUILT**
c. 1870
*Lancaster County, Pennsylvania*